CONTEMPORARY LIVES

BLAKE SHELTON

COUNTRY SINGER & TV PERSONALITY

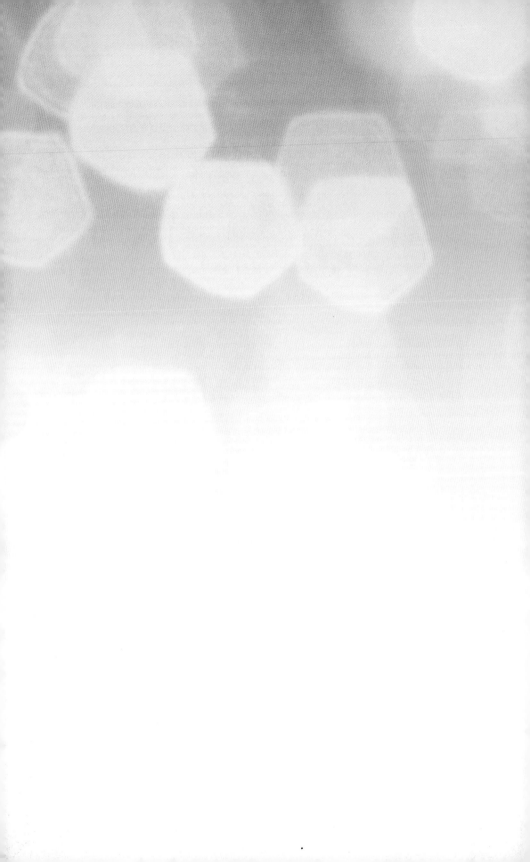

CONTEMPORARY LIVES

BLAKE SHELTON

COUNTRY SINGER & TV PERSONALITY

by Marcia Amidon Lusted

Essential Library

An Imprint of Abdo Publishing | www.abdopublishing.com

www.abdopublishing.com

Published by Abdo Publishing, a division of ABDO, PO Box 398166,
Minneapolis, Minnesota 55439. Copyright © 2015 by Abdo Consulting
Group, Inc. International copyrights reserved in all countries. No part of this
book may be reproduced in any form without written permission from the
publisher. Essential Library™ is a trademark and logo of Abdo Publishing.

Printed in the United States of America, North Mankato, Minnesota
092014
012015

Cover Photo: Helga Esteb/Shutterstock Images
Interior Photos: Helga Esteb/Shutterstock Images, 3; Amy Harris/
Corbis, 6–7, 83; Laura Farr/AdMedia/Corbis, 9; Chris Pizzello/Invision/
AP Images, 12, 86; Yearbook Library, 14–15, 19; Ed Rode/AP Images, 22;
Mark Humphrey/AP Images, 25, 97; Laura Farr/Zuma Press/Newscom,
26–27; Tim Mosenfelder/Corbis, 29; Curtis Hilbun/AP Images, 33, 96;
Donna Ward/ABACAUSA.COM/Newscom, 36–37; Angie Wagner/Retna Ltd./
Corbis, 41; Evan Agostini/AP Images, 44; Wade Payne/AP Images, 47, 97;
PatrickMcMullan.com/AP Images, 48–49, 98; Trae Patton/NBC/AP Images,
53; Matt Sayles/AP Images, 56; Splash News/Corbis, 59; Frank Micelotta/
Invision/AP Images, 60–61, 67, 98; Mike McCarn/AP Images, 63; John
Davisson/Invision/AP Images, 68–69, 100; Mario Anzuoni/Reuters/Corbis,
73; Evan Agostini/Invision/AP Images, 74; Brett Deering/NBC/AP Images,
78–79; PRNewsFoto/Atlantic City Alliance/AP Images, 88–89; Getty Images
Entertainment/Thinkstock, 95

Editor: Mirella Miller
Series Designer: Emily Love

Library of Congress Control Number: 2014943857

Cataloging-in-Publication Data

Lusted, Marcia Amidon.
 Blake Shelton: country singer & TV personality / Marcia Amidon Lusted.
  p. cm. -- (Contemporary lives)
Includes bibliographical references and index.
ISBN 978-1-62403-547-0
1. Shelton, Blake, 1976- --Juvenile literature. 2. Country musicians--United
States--Biography--Juvenile literature. 3. Singers--United States--Biography--
Juvenile literature.   1. Title.
782.421642092--dc23
[B]

2014943857

CONTENTS

Shelton performed at the
2012 CMA Music Festival in June.

CHAPTER 1
A Night
of Awards

||||||||||||||||||||||||||||||||||||||||||||||||||||

The crowd at the 2012 Country Music Association (CMA) Awards in Nashville, Tennessee, murmured as the nominees were read for Song of the Year. As music video clips from the five nominated songs were shown, nominees Blake Shelton and his wife, fellow country singer Miranda Lambert, sat patiently in the audience.

Country music has its roots in Appalachian Mountain fiddle players who made recordings in the early 1900s. But it wasn't until the 1920s that country music was recorded and listened to by a wider audience. Most music historians believe country music started in 1927, with artists such as Jimmie Rodgers and the Carter Family. Country music also includes the country western genre. It uses syncopated rhythms, steel guitars, and bigger bands. Mainstream country music is simpler and uses fewer instruments.

"And the CMA Award for Song of the Year goes to . . . " There was a pause as country singer Darius Rucker opened the envelope. " . . . 'Over You' by Miranda Lambert and Blake Shelton!"[1] The crowd erupted in cheers and applause as Lambert turned to Shelton and buried her face in his shoulder. Then she collected herself, and they made their way to the stage to accept their award. Lambert, already sobbing, gestured to Shelton to make the speech.

> I lost my brother in a car wreck when I was 14 years old, and later in life when I decided I wanted to be a country singer, my dad always told me, 'Son, you should write a song about your brother.' And I lost my dad in January, and it's so amazing

Although Shelton won other awards at the 2012 CMA Awards, winning Song of the Year with Lambert meant the most to him.

to me that tonight, even after he's gone, he's still right. I just needed the right person to write this song with, and the right person to sing it.[2]

The song's lyrics, which sound similar to a romantic breakup song, actually refer to Shelton's older brother, Richie, who died in a car accident on November 13, 1990. The lyric about "seeing it in stone" is where the song shifts meaning. "This is the line where people who thought this was a song about a love gone bad realize [it's about someone who died]," says Lambert.[3] The song was written by Lambert and Shelton and recorded by Lambert. It reached Number 1 on the country music charts, selling enough to earn platinum certification.

Winning 2012 Song of the Year may have seemed like the highest point Shelton could reach, but it was not the only award he won that night.

RICHIE SHELTON

Shelton and his brother were very close. "The guy was my hero," Shelton says. "Talk about worship— he was the coolest guy on earth."[4] His brother took him fishing and gave him his collection of old country music records. When Richie died, one of the most heart-wrenching things for Shelton was that Richie's girlfriend and her four-year-old son died as well.

Record albums that sell certain numbers of copies become certified as gold, platinum, or diamond. According to the Recording Industry Association of America (RIAA), an album that sells 500,000 copies earns gold certification. If it sells 1 million copies, it becomes a platinum record. With new methods of selling music, first with CDs and now downloads, music has become more widely available. People were buying more albums, so a new category was created: the diamond award. This award is for albums or singles that sell more than 10 million copies.[5]

Shelton was also awarded Entertainer of the Year and Male Vocalist of the Year. The awards were another step along the way for a country music career that took Shelton from the tiny town of Milburn, Oklahoma, to Nashville, and then to Hollywood, California.

|||||||||||||||||||||||||||||||||||||||||||||||||||||||

COUNTRY MUSIC AND *THE VOICE*

Shelton is one of the most popular country singers, with eight best-selling albums in just 12 years. That would be enough for most singers, but not Shelton. Since 2011, he has also been a coach on

Shelton has become one of the most popular country singers, with many awards and albums in his career.

In 2012, Shelton was featured as one of the Sexiest Men Alive in *People* magazine. Shelton wasn't very impressed at first. But he knows it made his mom proud. "But my favorite thing about it is that I know my mom, who cuts hair in Ada, Okla., will cut that page out of the magazine and tape it to her mirror and point it out to everybody who comes to the shop."[6]

the NBC reality television singing competition *The Voice*. In six seasons, he has coached three winning contestants.

Some performers fail when they move beyond the talent that made them famous, but in Shelton's case, his success on television has only added to his success in country music. Three platinum albums, four gold albums, and sixteen Number 1 singles later, Shelton's success as a country singer and television personality is due to hard work, perseverance, and a little bit of luck.

||||||||||

Blake loved singing and playing guitar from a young age.

CHAPTER 2

A Boy from Oklahoma

||||||||||||||||||||||||||||||||||||||||||||||||||||||||||||||||||

A da, Oklahoma's motto is "Small Town, Big Opportunity," and that motto fits Shelton very well. He was born in Ada on June 18, 1976, as Blake Tollison Shelton. His dad, Richard Shelton, was a used car dealer. His mom, Dorothy Shackleford, owned a beauty salon. Blake was the youngest of three children. His older sister, Endy, loved to dance and performed in talent pageants, while his older brother, Richie, was a champion at motocross.

Blake was an outdoor kid, according to his dad. "Blake was busy from daylight till dark," he said. "I had to put in a PA system in the house so I could holler at him when it was time to come home."[1] Blake was also always humming or singing.

Blake's mom noticed he had musical talent, so she decided he should also try pageants. When Blake was eight years old, Dorothy entered him in a talent show where he was the only boy competing against 50 girls. He didn't like the experience, mostly because he was embarrassed to be the only boy.

||||||||||||||||||||||||||||||||||||||||||||||||||||||||

MULTI HAIRSTYLE ||||||||||||||||||||||||||||||||||||||||||||||||||||||||||||||||||||||||||||||

Shelton has always been laid-back about his style, including his hair. Early in his career, Shelton sported a mullet. In this style, the hair is short on the top and long in the back. Shelton refused to cut his hair even though people told him it looked bad. "Nobody else in the world seems to think it was as awesome as I still think it was," Shelton said. At the time, he claimed, "Basically, it has gotten to the point where it is just a matter of pride. And I know it looks like crap, but it is just more fun to me to irritate people than cut my hair to satisfy them." Shelton didn't cut his hair until 2006.[2]

MUSICAL BEGINNINGS

There was more to Blake's talent than beauty pageants and singing around the house. By 12 years old, Blake had learned how to play the guitar. He decided to try his luck at a local country music festival. Blake amazed the audience, including his parents, with his performance. "I was shocked," his dad later said. "We had no idea he could sing."[3]

Tragedy struck Blake's family in November 1990, when his older brother, Richie, was killed in a car accident at the age of 24, along with his girlfriend and girlfriend's son. Blake remembered, "I was standing outside, waiting for a buddy to pick me up for school, and I heard all these ambulances go by. I didn't think anything of it."[4] After learning the news, Blake was devastated. Blake inherited Richie's collection of country records. "I just listened to them over and over again to feel like he was there," Blake said.[5] Blake credited Richie's death for his decision to pursue a music career.

Blake started playing as often as he could at bars, picnics, rodeos, and local clubs. The next steps in Blake's career were due to a series of lucky meetings. When he was 15 years old, Blake was hired to play regular performances at the McSwain Theatre in Ada. The theater hosted live music events.

> "I always loved music, even when I was very small. I don't even know where that came from. I mean, it wasn't like we grew up singing in the living room as a family every night or anything."[6]
>
> —BLAKE SHELTON

While performing at McSwain Theatre, Blake met Mae Boren Axton. Axton was well known in music circles for helping write the Elvis Presley song "Heartbreak Hotel." She was also known for helping new, talented musicians, including country singers Willie Nelson and Reba McEntire, rise in the world of country music. Her son, Hoyt Axton, was also a country singer-songwriter.

Axton was in the audience for a tribute show in her honor, where Blake sang. She told him after the show he had a shot at success in country music. "If you really want to take a shot at this country music

After finishing his senior year of high school, a young Blake pursued his dream in Nashville.

business . . . you better get to Nashville," Axton advised him.[7] Axton also lived in Nashville. Blake had already won the Denbo Diamond Award at age 16, the highest award given to a promising young Oklahoma singer-songwriter. It was clear Blake needed to move away from Ada if he wanted to seriously pursue his musical career.

Two weeks after graduating from high school in 1994, at 17 years old, Blake moved to Nashville. "It was always Nashville or bust for me," Blake

Demo recordings are songs created for reference, rather than release to the public. Artists and bands create them as samples of their music. They then send them to recording companies in the hope that the singer or band will be signed to the label and will be able to then record a full-length album for general release.

remembered.[8] "I think it was just understood that when I graduated, that was my destiny."[9] Blake knew he was meant to be a country singer. His family thought he would quickly get tired of Nashville and come back home.

WAITING AND WORKING IN NASHVILLE

Blake arrived in Nashville with not much more than a suitcase and a guitar. As soon as he arrived, he called Axton to let her know he was in Nashville. She immediately hired him as a handyman to paint her house. Axton also allowed Blake to live with her and her family. This gave him somewhere to stay and an income while he tried to break into country music. Hoyt was currently living with his mother too, so Blake had plenty of opportunities to play music with Hoyt and talk about the music business. This helped Blake stay motivated to pursue his dream.

Blake continued working for Axton, making a living doing odd jobs and auditioning and recording demo vocals as much as he could. His hard work would take a while to pay off. After seven years in Nashville, Blake came to the attention of Bobby Braddock, a songwriter and producer. He was looking for new talent. Another songwriter, Michael Kosser, told Braddock about Blake. Kosser called Braddock and played Blake's demo song over the phone.

Braddock met with Blake and Blake recorded several songs Braddock helped write, including one called "Austin." Then Braddock began talking

BOBBY BRADDOCK ||||||||||||||||||||||||||||||||||||||||||||||||||||||||||||

In addition to being the man who discovered Shelton, Bobby Braddock is one of the best-known and most prolific songwriters in country music. He is also a musician, but he is most famous for his ability to write hit songs for singers such as Tammy Wynette, Willie Nelson, the Statler Brothers, and Jerry Lee Lewis. He is a member of the Country Music Hall of Fame and the Nashville Songwriters Hall of Fame.

Songwriter Bobby Braddock in 2011

to record companies all over Nashville, trying to
interest them in signing Blake to their label.

MAKING RECORDS . . .
SLOWLY

In 1998, Giant Records signed Shelton. Once a
record label signs a new artist, the label and artist

begin working on an album. They pick an album theme and songs that will appear on the album. Shelton worked for three years before his debut album and single were released. Shelton's self-titled album, *Blake Shelton*, including the song "Austin," was released in 2001.

> "I said, 'The song's okay, but who's that guy singing? He [Kosser] said, 'That's the kid I was telling you about.'"[10]
>
> —BOBBY BRADDOCK ON LISTENING TO SHELTON

The timing was bad because Giant Records was about to go out of business. But Shelton was lucky because Fritz Kuhlman, a promoter for Giant, had sent Shelton's album to radio stations before Giant closed. It paid off. By the time Giant went out of business, "Austin" was already on the country music charts. It was in the Top 20 on the *Billboard* Hot 100 list. "Austin" spent five weeks in the Number 1 position.

This success caught Warner Brothers Records' attention. It signed Shelton to its label. Shelton's first single had hit Number 1, and his first album

Billboard Hot 100 creates many music charts that track the popularity of songs and albums in different genres. The chart ratings are based on fans and the music. This includes album sales and downloads, track downloads, radio airplay, and touring. It also includes social media interactions on sites such as Vevo, YouTube, and Spotify.

went to Number 3 on the charts. It eventually sold enough copies to go gold. It had taken seven years of struggle and hard work, but Shelton was now on his way to the musical career he'd dreamed of.

||||||||||

"Austin" became Shelton's first Number 1 hit on the *Billboard* country music chart.

Shelton's popularity continued growing as he released more albums and singles.

CHAPTER 3

Making His Way to the Top

‖‖‖

S helton had a hit single, a gold album, and a contract with Warner Brothers Records. But he still had a long way to go before he reached superstardom.

Shelton's next two albums, *The Dreamer* in 2003 and *Blake Shelton's Barn & Grill* in 2004, came in rapid succession. Shelton did not just sing on these albums. He also wrote and cowrote a few songs on both albums. Each album was fairly well received by critics. Robert L. Doerschuk reviewed *The Dreamer* for AllMusic, an online music guide, saying,

> *Rough, rawboned energy drives Blake Shelton's sophomore release, but it's not quite enough to distract from its brevity or the fact that the young singer would benefit from a little more seasoning. His vocal technique is fine, and his willingness to tackle a lyric is admirable.*[1]

Still, the album generated a Number 1 hit, "The Baby," and eventually sold enough to go gold.

Blake Shelton's Barn & Grill also went gold and produced another Number 1 single, "Some Beach." Three other songs on the album hit the Top 100

PET TURKEY

Shelton is known for his sense of humor and quirky habits. In 2003, Shelton told Country Music Television (CMT) he had a pet turkey named Turkey, and that he hoped to bring him to his next awards show. Shelton noted that Turkey had traveled to Arkansas and Oklahoma and lived in Tennessee, but had not been anywhere else. Shelton joked that it was his responsibility to show Turkey the world. Unfortunately, Turkey died of heat stroke before he could attend a show.

Shelton performs in 2003 as part of Toby Keith's Shock'n Y'All Tour.

and the Top 10 on the country music charts. A reviewer believed Shelton had trouble finding his signature style in his first two albums, but this album was a better mix.

To promote the albums and make sure they sold well, Shelton had a grueling schedule of 120 concerts in a year. All of the traveling started to get to Shelton. He later admitted he did not enjoy the concerts and did not give it his all each night.

Many music stars are given gifts by their fans on tours. Shelton is no exception. The oddest—and most startling—gift Shelton was ever given was an iguana. "We were playing a fair, and a few people were handing me stuffed animals and flowers, but one person handed me a paper sack," Shelton said. "So I took all the stuff back to the bus. I put the sack in my lap and opened it, and a live iguana jumped out of the sack and onto my shirt. I screamed like a little girl! I think it took a year off my life—it scared the [heck] out of me."[3]

Shelton toured with country superstar Toby Keith in 2003 as part of Keith's Shock'n Y'All Tour, but Shelton was a popular draw himself. One reviewer described his part of the concert:

> It was clear that Blake Shelton was a major draw for this concert, as the crowd leapt to their feet as he took the stage. Blake, too, wasted little time, getting right into the music with a crowd-pleasing performance of "Austin," his first hit single. . . . I had never been blown away by Blake's videos or singles, but let me tell you this: Blake is one [heck] of a performer and I now have a lot more respect for this great entertainer.[2]

A COUNTRY WEDDING

On November 17, 2003, Shelton celebrated a personal milestone. He married his road manager, Kaynette "Katt" Williams. Williams was also from Ada. She had known Shelton since she was 15 years old, but they didn't start dating until six years later. Shelton dated Williams for several years before proposing to her.

Williams and Shelton married in a very small, private ceremony in Gatlinburg, Tennessee. Only Williams, Shelton, the minister, and a photographer were in attendance. "Our whole lives are always in the public eye, plus we live on a bus with 10 other people. There's just always people around. We never have time for us, so it seemed like the perfect way to do this," Shelton said.[4]

IT STARTED WITH A DUET

For the first two years of their marriage, Shelton was touring and performing regularly, and Williams was his road manager. By most accounts, they were happy together. In 2005, the Country Music Television (CMT) network ran a special concert called 100 Greatest Duets. Newer country singers performed famous duets. For the concert, Shelton was paired with another up-and-coming country music singer, Miranda Lambert.

Lambert had performed on a weekly variety show in Arlington, Texas, and had done some acting work. She had been a contestant on the talent competition *Nashville Star* in 2003. The show was similar to *American Idol*, but performers sang only country music. They had to win over judges and call-in voters. While Lambert didn't win the competition, she did land a contract with Sony Music. Lambert's first album, *Kerosene*, went platinum after its release in 2005.

Lambert and Shelton met for the first time on stage for the 100 Greatest Duets rehearsal. Neither could deny there was an instant attraction between them. "I knew he was married," Lambert admitted. "It was my first duet with some other country star, and I didn't know if it was initial butterflies because of that . . . I don't know what it was. It was just this draw to each other."[5] She had no intention of starting a relationship with someone else's husband.

Shelton and Lambert perform as part of CMT's
"100 Greatest Duets" in 2005.

Shelton also felt their chemistry. "I've never had
that kind of experience with anybody," he said. "I
was a married guy, you know? Standing up there

and singing with somebody and going, 'Man, this shouldn't be happening."[6] Shelton and Lambert became friends, but because Shelton was still married, they did not have a romantic relationship.

> **"Looking back on that, I was falling in love with her, right there on stage."[7]**
>
> —BLAKE SHELTON ON SINGING WITH MIRANDA LAMBERT IN 2005

ENDINGS AND BEGINNINGS

While Shelton's personal life had become much more complicated, his career was still going strong. Shelton made his first television appearance besides award shows in 2005. Several of his songs were part of a television movie called *The Christmas Blessing*, starring actors Neil Patrick Harris and Rob Lowe. At the end of the movie, Shelton made a brief appearance as himself, playing his song "Nobody but Me." It would be one of his first experiences with television, but not his last.

Shelton officially split with Williams in February 2006. In their divorce papers, Williams claimed Shelton was guilty of "inappropriate marital conduct." They were married for three years. Many of Williams's friends were bitter on her behalf. They felt she had stood by Shelton during the rough years when he was establishing his career, but that he turned his back on her for Lambert. Shelton admitted he wasn't ready to be a husband. After the divorce, he began dating Lambert. They purchased adjoining ranches in Tishomingo, Oklahoma, making this their home base. Lambert and Shelton would soon realize the large roles they would play in each other's lives.

||||||||||

WORST TATTOO?

Shelton believes he has one of the worst tattoos in the world, which he drew himself and had a tattoo artist add to his left forearm. He loves to hunt, so the tattoo was supposed to be deer tracks, but many people who see it mistake it for ladybugs. He even had barbed wire added to the tattoo to make it look "more manly," but some of his friends still make fun of it.

Shelton released another album in 2007 and continued making television appearances on shows such as *Clash of the Choirs*.

CHAPTER 4

Startin' Fires and More

||||||||||||||||||||||||||||||||||||||||||||||||||||||

Relationships were not the only thing filling Shelton's time. The country singer continued making albums. His fourth album, called *Pure BS*, was released in early 2007. The album generated two Top 20 hits, "Don't Make Me" and "The More I Drink."

There were also more television appearances for Shelton in late 2007.

There are several different organizations that give out awards for country music. The ACM has its own set of awards, the most prestigious being Artist of the Decade and Entertainer of the Year, with other awards for vocalists, videos, songs, and albums. The CMA gives out awards in 12 categories, including vocalists, songs, New Artist of the Year, videos, music events, and a broadcasting award. The Grammy Awards, which are industry wide, have a specific category for country music, as do the American Music Awards.

He appeared as a judge on *Nashville Star*, the same program on which Lambert got her start.

Shelton also appeared on the show *Clash of the Choirs*. This reality talent show miniseries featured choirs with people who lived in the hometowns of celebrity singers. The people competed against each other. The celebrity singers appeared on the show and supported the choirs. Shelton's choice from Oklahoma City, Oklahoma, came in third place in the four-night competition. The show only lasted one season. However, these television appearances would lead Shelton to another opportunity, one that would cement his position as a celebrity country music singer.

MORE ALBUMS

Pure BS was rereleased in 2008 with three bonus tracks. It supplied Shelton with his fourth Number 1 hit, a cover version of jazz singer Michael Bublé's hit song "Home." He followed this with another Number 1 single, "She Wouldn't Be Gone," which gave him two consecutive Number 1 hits.

Shelton's next album in 2008 was called *Startin' Fires*. It features a duet with Lambert, now his girlfriend, called "Bare Skin Rug." The album also produced two singles. As with all of Shelton's albums, the songs are a mix of things he wrote himself, songs written by others, and cover songs. It was clear Shelton was perfecting his ability to select or write songs that would have wide appeal and end up high on the charts.

Shelton was also gaining a reputation for his use of social media, especially Twitter. He posted frequently about what he was doing, and his playful, silly style attracted followers and made his fans feel a connection to him. Shelton would use Twitter and Facebook more and more to further his career and widen his fan base.

THE GRAND OLE OPRY

Shelton reached another milestone in September 2010. During the Country Comes Home concert at the Grand Ole Opry in Nashville, Shelton was invited to join the organization. The Grand Ole Opry is a weekly stage show and concert, broadcast on the radio, dedicated to country music and its history. The show has a large number of radio and Internet listeners, and its theater is a tourist attraction. The Grand Ole Opry is a symbol of country music and its history. Membership in the Opry is one of the crowning achievements for any country musician.

However, Shelton's invitation was a little unusual. He was invited to join via Twitter. During the concert show, country singer and Opry member Trace Adkins held up Shelton's phone. "You know Blake is famous for doing the Twitter thing; he's always sending tweets," Adkins said. "Well, the Grand Ole Opry sent Blake a tweet tonight." As he handed the phone to Shelton, a tweet popped up: "@blakeshelton, you're invited to join the Grand Ole Opry. See you on 10/23/2010!" Shelton immediately tweeted back: "Hmmm... Let me think...OK!!!!!!!"[1] Shelton was formally

Grand Ole Opry @opry

@blakeshelton, you're invited to join the Grand Ole Opry! See you on 10/23/10.

650 WSM · GRAND OLE OPRY www.O

Shelton, *center*, receives a tweet from the Grand Ole Opry inviting him to be its newest member in 2010.

inducted into the Opry on October 23, 2010. During this performance, he recorded the title track for the remake of the movie *Footloose*, which was released in 2011. This live version was used in the movie.

AWARDS AND MORE AWARDS

Life was going well for Shelton. After his Grand Ole Opry induction, he released his first greatest hits album in November 2010. Shelton also continued receiving awards for his music. The Academy of Country Music (ACM) had nominated Shelton for Top New Male Vocalist in 2001 and 2002, and his song "The Truth about Men" had been nominated for Vocal Event of the Year in 2003. But his first win came in 2010 when he was nominated for Vocal Event of the Year for the song "Hillbilly Bone," sung with Trace Adkins. Shelton won a variety of other awards as well, including the 2010 CMT Video of the Year for "Hillbilly Bone" and the 2010 Country Music Association (CMA) Male Vocalist of the Year.

A TEXAS WEDDING

Shelton proposed to Lambert in 2010. Lambert said, "He asked me at our ranch. I was in a camo jacket. That should tell you all you need to know about that."[2] Shelton had even asked Lambert's father for permission to marry her before asking and researched rings. "I was so proud of him," Miranda added. "We've been together five years, so he knew exactly what [ring] I wanted but it's so much more perfect than I could have picked out myself."[3] Lambert and Shelton were married on May 14, 2011, in Boerne, Texas. Many country music celebrities were there. Despite Shelton's reputation for clowning around and being silly, Lambert's mother, Bev, said, "Blake was staring so hard at Miranda when he was saying his vows. He said it like he meant it. He wasn't stumbling around or being funny."[4] After the ceremony, Shelton said, "When I see my mom and dad with their grandkids and that relationship down the road, that's what I'm looking forward to more than anything: that family and those generations and being on that end of things."[5]

Lambert and Shelton had a happy marriage and a good musical partnership. In 2010, Shelton's producer, Scott Hendricks, was looking for the perfect song that would push Shelton to the next musical level. He felt he had found that song, "The House That Built Me," and passed it along to

FAVORITE GIFTS

Shelton's favorite gifts given to him and Lambert for their engagement included matching his and hers shotguns. "We were outside the city limits, so we went right out of the tent and tried them out. It's a real shotgun wedding!" Lambert said.[6]

Now husband and wife, Shelton and Lambert celebrate their 2011 CMA Awards.

Shelton. The song became the 2011 CMA Song of the Year, but not for Shelton. He let Lambert record the song, because hearing it had moved her to tears and she really wanted to sing it. As a result, she won the award.

RED RIVER BLUE

Shelton's career was not slowing down. In 2011, he released his album *Red River Blue*, including a single called "Honey Bee." That song received 138,000 downloads in its first week and went gold in its seventh week.[7] This was a new record for a song by a male country singer. In its tenth week, "Honey Bee" reached Number 1 on the *Billboard* Hot Country Songs chart. *Red River Blue* kept taking over the charts, as the album debuted at Number 1 on the *Billboard* 200 chart. Critics gave the album good reviews, calling it "the perfect summertime sound track, a mix of rollicking honky-tonk stomps and breezy mid-tempo tunes, all steeped in Shelton's considerable twangy charm."[8]

Red River Blue also spawned three more hit singles, "God Gave Me You," "Drink on It," and

"Over." These songs all hit Number 1 on the charts, and "Drink on It" was his sixth consecutive Number 1. Shelton was still writing only a small percentage of his songs at this point, however, relying on other songwriters to create material for him.

Shelton went on to win the 2011 CMA Male Vocalist of the Year and 2011 Favorite Country Male Artist from the American Music Awards. He would continue to accumulate nominations and wins from many different music awards shows. But as Shelton put it, "I'm still learning, still reaching and growing, and it's great to have more and more people along for the ride."[9] And the ride was getting more and more interesting, but not without its ups and downs.

||||||||||

Shelton performs in 2011 at
CMA Fan Fest in Nashville.

In 2011, Shelton signed on to be a coach on reality television show *The Voice*.

CHAPTER 5

The Voice

IIIIIIIIIIIIIIIIIIIIIIIIIIIIIIIIIIIIIIIIIIIIIIIIIIIIIIIIIIII

O n April 26, 2011, a new reality television singing competition premiered on the NBC network. It was based on a Dutch talent show called *The Voice of Holland*. Retitled *The Voice* for US audiences, the show was different from other popular singing competitions, such as *American Idol*. During the audition phase, the coaches did not see the contestants. The contestants were judged on their singing, not their appearance or style. The coaches were singers, rather than producers or music executives, and they represented a range of music genres. Viewers and coaches voted for the winner on *The Voice*. The winner would receive $100,000 and a record deal with Universal Republic.

TAPPED TO BE A JUDGE

With his own career well established and growing steadily, Shelton was asked to be a coach on the first season of *The Voice*. Shelton had previously claimed he hated reality shows. But when he heard singer Christina Aguilera had signed on for the show, he decided not to be the holdout. He felt if she was comfortable being on the show, then it was a good career move for him as well. Shelton felt his success as a country singer was partly due to the fact that performers like him weren't usually seen in the New York and Los Angeles worlds of network television. He hoped to find more performers similar to him. Shelton said, "I'm the country guy nobody's ever heard of. . . . If there's one thing special about me, it's that I seem familiar. People feel like I live next door."[1]

From the start, Shelton was a success on the show, not only in mentoring contestants but also in growing his reputation with people outside the country music world. Shelton quickly became not only popular and successful on *The Voice*, but almost indispensable, according to some television critics. Brittany Frederick of Starpulse.com summed it up:

> *Coaching on* The Voice *isn't just about being one of "the biggest names in music," to quote host Carson Daly. It's also about being a TV personality that can entertain America and have*

A LYRIC CONTROVERSY ||||||||||||||||||||||||||||||||||||||||||||||||||||||

During a performance by the Seattle Starbucks' Chorus on an episode of *The Voice*, the words to the classic gospel hymn "Will the Circle Be Unbroken" were changed to eliminate the word "Lord" from the song, replacing it with "Oh." Shelton did not realize the lyric change had been made until fans angrily tweeted about it. He said, "I don't know what, how it happened, I'm learning about it just like you guys are. I was sitting in my chair singing that song how I grew up on it, with 'in the sky, Lord, in the sky.' . . . I know . . . it's meant for a good cause, and they're trying to raise some money. And that's a good thing. But I will say, that's not the version I grew up on. And that's not the version I was singing sitting in my chair, if that clears up anything [about] where I stand on this thing."[2]

a good rapport with the other panelists. More important than that, it's about being the best possible mentor for a dozen would-be singers. And being able to commit to weeks of coaching, live tapings, and press appearances. Finding somebody who fits all those criteria is an uphill battle. Not only [does] . . . Blake tick off all those boxes, it's pretty clear that [he's] set the standard for what a coach on The Voice should be.[3]

It was also a very lucrative job for Shelton. He was paid approximately $4 million per season.

A GREAT TRACK RECORD

Shelton developed a great track record coaching on *The Voice*. In his first season, his contestant, Dia Frampton, came in second place. In Seasons 2, 3, and 4, the winners all came from Shelton's team. And in Season 3, the runner-up was also from Shelton's team. In Season 5, however, the contestant he coached came in third place.

Not only was Shelton making a name for himself on television and helping to make the show popular, he was also mentoring a new generation

Season 4 winner Danielle Bradbury poses with coach Shelton after the finale.

Shelton and Lambert are known for their generosity, as one of the contestants on *The Voice*, Dia Frampton, knows firsthand. The dress she wanted to wear for the finale was too expensive for her wardrobe budget. Frampton arrived the day of the finale wondering what she would wear. She quickly found out Shelton and Lambert had bought the dress she wanted. Frampton said, "That's how they are, they are so genuine."[5]

of singers. Sometimes it was difficult for Shelton to stay detached from the singers he was helping:

> Especially whenever you've been in the rehearsals with them and you've had all these conversations with them that are about why they want to do this and that. And next thing you know, you're friends with them and you're talking to them all the time and see them and you want this for them as badly as they do.[4]

Shelton tries to promote the past winners from *The Voice* and other singers he believes have real talent. He has even taken past contestants on tour with him.

|||||||||||||||||||||||||||||||||||||||||||||||||||||||||||||

TEAMWORK AND FUN

In addition to judging on *The Voice*, Shelton frequently performs on the show. He has been able to sing duets with some of his fellow coaches, such as Latin music singer Shakira. During Season 5 in 2013, the two performed the country song "Need You Now" during the show. Shakira had so much fun she told Shelton she wanted to write a country song herself. She did, and Shelton performed the song, "Medicine," with her on her tenth album, released in March 2014. The pair also performed the song at the 2014 ACM Awards.

"I always felt that if the TV cameras discovered Blake, they would fall in love with him. He's so funny. He's got a great personality for TV."[6]

—*BOBBY BRADDOCK*

During Season 6 in 2014, Shelton and fellow judge Adam Levine managed to have some fun with each other through a series of practical jokes. It started as a series of tweets during one of the live shows. Shelton tweeted Levine's phone number,

Levine and Shelton are good friends who enjoy having fun on and off the set of *The Voice*.

which sparked a good-natured back-and-forth between the two. It ended with Levine arranging to have a load of manure dumped on Shelton's prized pickup truck.

But these on-air pranks serve to soothe the nerves of the contestants. The Levine/Shelton incidents also show how the judges interact on a personal level. Fellow judge Usher said, "We really do care about one another and though this is a competition and everybody obviously wants to win, we're enjoying it while we're doing it."[7]

Shelton was slated to continue on Season 7 of *The Voice* in the fall of 2014. He and Levine help with the show's continuing success. As Starpulse. com said:

> Blake has shown the ability to nurture talent, particularly the less experienced artists, which is crucial as The Voice's talent pool seems to skew younger every season. All of the coaches can do the job, but [Shelton and Levine] operate on another level. That extends to what they do off-camera, too. Both Adam and Blake have maintained relationships with their Voice artists well after their time on the show has

Many countries around the world, from Afghanistan to Vietnam, have their own versions of *The Voice* television show. Many of them feature children and are called *The Voice Kids* or *The Voice Junior.*

ended. They've gone above and beyond the call of duty here. And that's also made them great ambassadors for The Voice. *Ask any former Team Adam or Team Blake member and they'll not only tell you about what they learned from a coaching standpoint, but praise their coaches for being amazing people.*[8]

But Shelton was not content to appear simply as a coach on *The Voice*. His own career continued to climb, too, even when his personal life got rough.

IIIIIIIIII

The Voice judges gather before the start of season 5 in 2013.

Lambert and Shelton perform
at Super Bowl XLVI together.

CHAPTER 6

In the Public Eye

||||||||||||||||||||||||||||||||||||||||||||||||||||

While Shelton's *Voice* appearances were bringing him more mainstream popularity, he was still growing personally and professionally. On January 17, 2012, Shelton's father, Richard, died of lung disease in Shawnee, Oklahoma. Because his father was ill for a long time and it was clear he would not recover, Shelton was there when he passed away. Richard got to hear Shelton's song "Over You," about Richie and see it released, although he did not live to see it win Song of the Year. "So he got to see it going up the charts," Shelton said. "That was pretty cool."[1] Shelton was glad his father had lived long enough to see Shelton write a song about his brother. After his father's death, Shelton canceled a number of tour dates. On his website he wrote, "I appreciate your understanding during this difficult time and thank you for all your prayers. Your support means the world to me. I love you guys."[2]

When Shelton was ready to perform again, he and Lambert continued to work together.

A VOICE FROM HOME

A few weeks after Shelton moved to Nashville at 17 years old, he received a letter in the mail from his dad. It was five pages long and contained things his dad hadn't had a chance to tell him about the real world. Shelton set it aside unread and didn't think about it again until after his dad died. A few days after his dad's death, Shelton found the letter and read it for the first time. Some of it was practical information. "But there was also a lot of [stuff] about how to treat people," Shelton said, "how to get respect, how to look people in the eye, and how to shake their hand—basically, how to be a man in the world. It was like I was having a conversation with him I never had."[3]

Shelton performs at the 2012 NASCAR Sprint Cup
All-Star auto race in North Carolina.

On February 5, 2012, they sang a duet version of
"America the Beautiful" during Super Bowl XLVI.
It was their first television appearance since they
were married.

Shelton also completed his sold-out arena tour,
Well Lit & Amplified, just after the Super Bowl
appearance. Shelton's popularity had risen so high
that he was able to sell out large arenas. The *Saint*

Louis Post-Dispatch said Shelton did a great job creating a fan-friendly show with a mix of songs and stories.

Shelton was busy throughout 2012, performing at the 2012 CMA Music Festival in Nashville. He also performed during the 2012 Country Music Awards show. Shelton had an impressive list of nominations for the CMT Awards, including Video of the Year and Male Video of the Year for "God Gave Me You," and CMT Performance of the Year for *Footloose*. He did not win in any of these categories, but a few months later he did win big at the CMA Awards, winning Entertainer of the Year, Male Vocalist of the Year, and Song of the Year for "Over You." It was a special night for Shelton. He took the chance to reflect on his dreams when he first moved to Nashville, saying, "When I moved to Nashville in 1994, I had two goals. One was to someday have a gold record, and the other was to be a member of the Country Music Hall of Fame. But, Entertainer of the Year? Wow."[4]

Shelton celebrated the 2012 holidays with another new album, *Cheers, It's Christmas*. The album features several duet performances with entertainers such as Michael Bublé and Reba

McEntire, as well as one with his mother, Dorothy. His mom was not a professional singer, but Shelton sang with her for fun. Shelton had released a successful version of Bublé's song "Home" in 2008. For this Christmas album, he and Bublé reworked the song to represent the Christmas spirit and the importance of homecomings for the holidays. His duet with his mother, "Time for Me to Come Home," captures the longing of a son who was on the road to go home to his family for Christmas. The album hit Number 1 on *Billboard's* Top Holiday Albums and Number 2 on the Top Country Albums chart.

As 2012 came to a close, Shelton had accumulated 12 Number 1 hit singles. Each hit

NOT SO FAMILY CHRISTMAS ||||||||||||||||||||||||||||||||||||||||||||||||||

In 2012, Shelton had his first Christmas special on television. Called "Blake Shelton's Not So Family Christmas," it featured Shelton and Lambert, as well as guest appearances from Reba McEntire, Jay Leno, Kelly Clarkson, Christina Aguilera, and Shelton's mother, Dorothy. The show was an old-fashioned variety show, with music and skits, intended to be funny and lighthearted. It featured a claymation spoof where Shelton and a friend go hunting and accidentally shoot Rudolph the Red-Nosed Reindeer.

When Shelton appeared on the documentary *Backstory* in 2012, he made some comments about country music and the direction in which it was heading. "Country music has to evolve in order to survive. Nobody wants to listen to their grandpa's music," Shelton said.[5] His comments angered many country music fans, who wanted him fired from the Grand Ole Opry. Eventually the incident blew over.

single since 2007 had debuted within the Top Ten. He had also been nominated for or won many of the most prestigious awards in both the country music industry and the music industry as a whole. He ended the year with a special about his life on the Great American Country channel's critically acclaimed *Backstory* series. He shared his life story of growing up in Oklahoma and moving to Nashville at 17 years old. He also shared his struggles in the industry and personal struggles with tragedy and divorce. After so much success and acclaim in 2012, what would the next year bring for Shelton?

|||||||||||

Shelton performs onstage at the 2012 Grammy Awards.

2013 would prove to be
another big year for Shelton.

CHAPTER 7

Based on a True Story . . .

||||||||||||||||||||||||||||||||||||||||||||||||||||||||||||||||||||||||||||||||

Shelton started 2013 with a new album and more chart-topping singles. Just after midnight on New Year's Day, he released the single "Sure Be Cool If You Did," which reached Number 1 on the *Billboard* Hot Country Songs and Country Airplay chart. Critics liked the song. The song preceded the release of Shelton's new album, *Based on a True Story…*, which was released in March 2013.

It debuted at Number 1 on the country chart and Number 3 on the general music chart. One critic said, "People have said of Blake's album that 'Like him, it's just all so dang likeable.'"[1] The album, like most of Shelton's previous albums, resulted in a total of four Number 1 singles. The fourth single, "Doin' What She Likes," was Shelton's eleventh consecutive Number 1 single, breaking the record previously held by country singer Brad Paisley since 2009.

Shelton also appeared in a special show in Nashville in February. Singer Sheryl Crow hosted a special performance for a select audience at the exclusive Tuesday Night Country Club called "Sheryl Crow and Friends." Both Shelton and Lambert performed during the show. Crow

A LITERARY MOM

In 2013, Shelton's mother, Dorothy, published a book called *Time for Me to Come Home*. The Christmas story echoes Shelton's life, with a main character who is a successful country music star but realizes the only place he wants to be for Christmas is home in Oklahoma. The book is based on the song "Time for Me to Come Home," written by Dorothy and Shelton, which debuted on Shelton's *Cheers, It's Christmas* album.

also surprised Shelton with a special plaque to commemorate the album *Red River Blue* reaching platinum status.

AN IMPORTANT WIN

In 2013, Shelton was chosen for a special honor by the ACM. He received the Gene Weed Special Achievement Award, which is an award that honors unprecedented, unique, and outstanding achievement by a country music performer. Previous recipients included Garth Brooks, George Burns, Jeff Foxworthy, Willie Nelson, and George Strait. According to Great American Country, Shelton received the award largely for his work on *The Voice*:

> *Blake Shelton stepped into his role on NBC's* The Voice *as a well-known figure in country music circles. Now he's a household name to millions of viewers who appreciate his lively personality, his honest approach toward aspiring talent and his camaraderie with pop stars like Christine Aguilera, Cee Lo Green and Adam Levine.*[2]

In his acceptance speech for the award, Shelton was unusually sincere, since his speeches were often irreverent and playful. "When you get going in this business, sometimes you don't take the time to stop and look around and see how lucky you are," he said. "In 1994, Mae Axton encouraged me to move to Nashville, and I was completely obsessed with country music. All I dreamed about was wanting to be one of them. 20 years later, and I have all these friends. I got to be one of them—at least for a minute."[3]

From July through October 2013, Shelton went nationwide on his Ten Times Crazier Tour. The tour kicked off in Virginia Beach, Virginia. Shelton commented, "I'm excited to be on stage with my band playing some of our new songs off *Based On A True Story*… and also getting to play some older hits that haven't been in our set over recent years."[4] The tour sold out its first three weekends, with fans camping out in parking lots before the concerts. Even Shelton was surprised.

I went outside and realized my fans had arrived earlier in the morning to tailgate. Here we are in New York and there are pickup trucks and cowboy

Shelton performs his hit
"Sure Be Cool If You Did" at
the 2013 ACM Awards.

Rumors continued to swirl
about Shelton and Lambert's
marriage and personal life.

Despite the constant rumors of separation and divorce, Lambert says the couple's relationship is as strong as ever. She wonders how the tabloids come up with their stories. But she also agrees the constant attention makes things tough. "It's not easy when everyone is trying to tear you down, but you make a commitment and you stick to it. . . . But country has some enduring marriages—Johnny and June, George and Nancy, Faith and Tim. I'm thankful we have those role models," Lambert said.[6]

hats filling out the parking lot at Jones Beach. That was beyond anything I had anticipated.[5]

The concerts were well reviewed everywhere Shelton performed.

||||||||||||||||||||||||||||||||||||||||||||||||||||

RUMORS . . . OR NOT?

While Shelton's musical career was continuing to climb, rumors began circulating about the health of his marriage to Lambert. Starting in 2013, tabloid journalists and gossip websites began repeatedly claiming the two were about to split. Others claimed Lambert had given Shelton an ultimatum about cleaning up his act—he was supposedly

Lambert is no stranger to winning awards for her music. As of April 2014, she had won five consecutive ACM Female Vocalist of the Year Awards, giving her the record for the most consecutive wins in that category. She has also won numerous awards from other country music awards organizations, *Billboard* Music awards, and one Grammy Award.

drinking and partying too much—or she would leave him. Other sources claimed Lambert was pregnant, or that she refused to have a baby until Shelton shaped up. But unlike many celebrities, who might ignore these kinds of rumors or address them seriously, Shelton and Lambert chose to take them lightly and laugh them off.

Given Shelton's love for social media sites such as Twitter, that was one way Lambert and Shelton addressed the rumors. "Me and @mirandalambert are reading about our separation," Shelton tweeted after a celebrity weekly magazine cover claimed "it's over." "I hope I get all the liquor in the divorce!!!"[7]

However, during an interview with Carson Daly on the *Today* show, Shelton was more serious:

I would take this opportunity to say, to clear the air, you may pick up a magazine or a tabloid any day of the week that'll say something about my relationship with Miranda, and that it's in turmoil and we're gonna divorce. And the truth is, I've never felt a stronger bond . . . not only with her but with any other human being in my life. I mean, Miranda and I, she's my life.[8]

Rumors about their marriage and the chances of the couple having a baby continued to surface in the tabloid media regularly. Then an event took place on May 20, 2013, that would ultimately show there was yet another side to Shelton besides being a popular entertainer.

||||||||||

TWITTER

Shelton is a dedicated user of Twitter. In fact, he has more than 500,000 followers, and he routinely stays in touch with his fans that way. "It's fun because I can instantly have contact with my fans and talk to them and argue with them and laugh with them," he says. "That's the relationship I wanted to create with my fan base. I don't want to be standoffish or fake."[9]

Shelton helped organize a benefit concert for the town of Moore, Oklahoma, in 2013.

CHAPTER 8

Healing in the Heartland

|||||||||||||||||||||||||||||||||||||||||||||||||||||||||||||||||||||||||||

O n May 20, 2013,
tornado-warning sirens
sounded in the town of
Moore, Oklahoma. Sixteen minutes later,
one of the biggest tornadoes in the state's
history cut a one-mile- (1.6 km) wide
swath through the town. The tornado
was a category EF5 on the Enhanced
Fujita scale used to measure tornadoes.
An EF5 storm has a wind speed of more
than 200 miles per hour (320 kmh). It is

the strongest measurable tornado, according to the National Oceanic and Atmospheric Administration (NOAA). Twenty-five people died in Moore, including seven children who were killed when the walls of their elementary school collapsed on them.[1] Many homes and buildings in Moore were completely flattened, and the town was covered in debris. Volunteers spent days searching for survivors trapped in the wreckage.

A CONCERT FOR RELIEF

Moore is only 74 miles (119 km) from Ada, and almost immediately after the storm, Shelton began planning a benefit concert to raise money to aid the people impacted by the tornado. Shelton had a personal connection to Moore. His sister used to live in one of the neighborhoods obliterated by the tornado. "I spent three Christmases there," he said. "That elementary school [where seven children were killed] is the one my niece would have been at."[3]

Shelton found a producer for the concert and began lining up musicians to perform. He had very specific ideas about what he wanted the concert to be. He wanted the concert to be heartwarming and to feature other country artists from Oklahoma, including Carrie Underwood, Garth Brooks, and Toby Keith.

The concert, called Healing in the Heartland, took place on May 29 in Oklahoma City, Oklahoma. It was televised on the NBC network. Tickets to the event sold out just minutes after they went on sale, filling the 20,000-seat arena. In addition to the performers Shelton wanted, other performers included Usher, Shelton and Lambert, Reba McEntire, Vince Gill, Luke Bryan, Joe Don Rooney, Rascal Flatts, and Ryan Tedder of OneRepublic. The one-hour concert raised more than $6 million for relief efforts.[4] Shelton and Usher closed the concert with a duet performance of the Michael Bublé song "Home." "People have

EMOTIONAL CONCERT ||||||||||||||||||||||||||||||||||||||||||||||||||||||

Shelton knew the best way to help the tornado victims and raise money was by touching donors' hearts. The Healing in the Heartland concert was extremely emotional. Lambert broke down in tears when images of victims were shown. Fans felt the emotions, too. They shared on Twitter how Lambert and other artists' reactions showed how devastating the Moore tornadoes had been.

given so much to us over the years and it's times like this when you can give back," Shelton told reporters before the event. "You have to. It's not a question of 'will you?' You have to step up."[5]

Shelton's public service efforts were not limited to the Healing in the Heartland concert. In December 2013, he teamed up with retailer J. C. Penney to produce a commercial that featured him singing "Silent Night" with United Service Organizations (USO) families in the background. The USO supports members of the military and their families. They often put on concerts and other kinds of entertainment for troops stationed all over the world. As part of the promotion, Shelton appeared in a concert at the J. C. Penney store in the Manhattan Mall in New York City. He sang "Silent Night" along with a chorus of USO singers. For every customer who uploaded a video of them singing the song, J. C. Penney made a donation to the USO, resulting in more than $1 million in contributions.[6]

On May 20, 2014, Shelton and Lambert both participated in a two-hour ACM Salute to the Troops concert televised on CBS, along with many other country music stars. The concert featured

Over the years, Shelton has
donated his time to charities
including the USO.

members of the US Armed Forces performing onstage with the celebrity musicians. Joe Montegna, a concert presenter, said the reason the concert was so cool was that well-known, popular country music performers teamed up with active members of the military who could sing or play an instrument. It made the military performers the stars of the show, and the famous musicians took a backseat.

ON THE ROAD AGAIN

Shelton's own popularity continued to surge. He announced he would be doing a 22-concert tour in the summer of 2014, called the Ten Times Crazier 2014 Tour. The tour would kick off in June in Austin, Texas, and would cover cities on the West Coast and in the Midwest. Shelton was excited to be on tour again, saying,

> I cannot wait to get back out on the road. I had so much fun playing songs from Based On A True Story . . . and getting to see the crowd's reaction to those songs was unforgettable. It is one of the most validating things for an artist like me, to have people sing along to your songs . . .

it means what I'm doing is right and no matter what I'm doing, whether it is The Voice or a TV special, absolutely nothing compares to playing live for me.[7]

Shelton also announced that $1 from every fan club presale ticket for the tour would be donated to the ACM Lifting Lives foundation, which tries to improve lives through the power of music.

> "He is witty, tall and has beautiful eyes. He can do all the macho things—hunt, fish, drive a truck—but with a woman, he's a sweetheart."[8]
>
> —REBA MCENTIRE, ON BLAKE SHELTON

Shelton's tour was a success before the first concert was even performed: concerts at both Madison Square Garden in New York City and the Hollywood Bowl in Los Angeles sold out in March 2014. It was Shelton's first time as the lead act in both venues, and he was thrilled by the response to his upcoming concerts. "Its mind blowing to think I'm performing at Madison Square Garden and the Hollywood Bowl let alone selling them out.

Shelton and Shakira perform at the 2014 ACM Awards.

I'm incredibly thankful for my fans selling out both these shows so fast."[9]

Shelton was also chosen to cohost the 2014 ACM Awards, where he would also perform.

He performed a duet of the song "Medicine" with Shakira. At the same time, his sixteenth Number 1 single, "Doin' What She Likes" from his *Based on a True Story* . . . album, became his eleventh consecutive top single, setting yet another new record for consecutive hit country songs. Shelton and his cohost Luke Bryan were one of the highlights of the show as they joked about celebrities and each performed two songs.

Clearly Shelton's career is continuing to accelerate, and his popularity has remained high. But as he became involved in new projects and endorsements, would his down-home demeanor and his philosophy remain the same?

||||||||||

LIFTING LIVES ||||||||||||||||||||||||||||||||||||||||||||||||||||||||||||||||||||||||||||||||||||

The Lifting Lives foundation helps improve people's lives through music. They partner with many different musical artists. ACM Lifting Lives creates and funds music-related therapy and education programs. The foundation helps communities with disaster relief, but they also bring music education and camps to schools and veterans.

New opportunities continued
to arise for Shelton in 2014.

CHAPTER 9

Looking Forward

⠀⠀⠀⠀⠀⠀⠀⠀⠀⠀⠀⠀⠀⠀⠀⠀⠀⠀⠀⠀⠀⠀⠀⠀⠀

"All Oklahomans are entertainers . . . feed store humor, commonsense intellect, charisma . . . we get it, and there's always an audience for that when it's combined with a special talent."[1] Shelton spoke these words in an interview with *Distinctly Oklahoma Magazine* in 2010. Shelton has always held firm to his Oklahoma roots, even in the midst of show business and the world

Even though Shelton is a musician and television star, he loves returning to his Oklahoma ranch and experimenting with growing crops. He likes to spend his weekends driving around his property on a four-wheeler, spraying crops for weeds and planting new crops. "But alfalfa's just little tiny seeds, so you can plant it and hope it don't wash away. I'm better at soybeans, squash, corn—stuff you can't really [mess] up."[3]

of a television celebrity. Shelton also maintains that keeping his roots and his philosophy out in the open is part of what makes him popular, and that it's necessary to his career. "For the life of me," he said, "I'll never understand how you can be an artist but not want people to understand who you are as a person."[2]

NEW OPPORTUNITIES

In 2014, Shelton had several new opportunities come his way, both in his career and in his small-town Oklahoma life. Oklahoma was, and still is, his home base, and he returns there with Lambert as often as possible. In May, Pizza Hut announced Shelton would be the new celebrity face of a line of barbecue pizzas the chain was introducing. One of the new flavors, "Blake's Smokehouse," is even named after him. Shelton claims he really does like these pizzas and it's not purely an endorsement deal for him. "I'm actually a fan of this idea, barbecue pizza," Shelton said. "I'm having a lot of fun working with the Pizza Hut people. They're so much fun to be around. Their headquarters is in Dallas, and that's basically right outside of where I live anyway, so we already have a lot in common."[4]

Close to home, in the small town of Tishomingo, Oklahoma, Shelton and Lambert are opening a bed-and-breakfast. Lambert

PIZZA NAMES

Shelton has tried to take an active interest in the new line of Pizza Hut pizzas he is endorsing. He sat down with the Pizza Hut chef to brainstorm names for the new pizzas. He realizes the pizza company may not like his ideas, so he gets creative and throws out rhymes. "Cutie fruity . . . the aloha bro-ha." His favorite pizza name? One named after him, of course. "The 'Shellshocked!' It's the first part of my last name but then you get into how shocking it is."[5]

already owned a clothing and antique shop in town, and she bought a two-story neighboring building. Shelton recalled reading in the tabloids that Lambert planned to turn it into a bed-and-breakfast. He agreed to help. The bed-and-breakfast was set to open in the fall of 2014. Shelton and Lambert hoped to attract guests who drive to Tishomingo to shop at Lambert's clothing store.

"Blake is just Blake. When he's around us, he's as common as anybody can be. We lose track, really, of just how big he's become."[6]

—RICHARD SHELTON, BLAKE'S DAD, IN 2011

As far as his music goes, Shelton continues to write and sing hit songs, tour, and stay true to his country roots. His eleventh album, *Bringing Back the Sunshine*, was released in September 2014. Even though Shelton has signed on for Season 7 of *The Voice*, he is still a musician first and foremost and is committed to his music, despite offers to appear in movies and more frequently on television.

ALWAYS AN OKLAHOMAN

No matter what new places his career takes him, at the end of the day Shelton will always return to Oklahoma. Shelton keeps a private jet in the airstrip near his home, where he parks his truck. As soon as he's done shooting *The Voice* on Wednesdays, he flies back to Oklahoma, where doing the regular things that regular people do there refreshes him:

> *A hot date means throwing a cooler in the back of the pickup and driving around the property clearing brush and singing to the radio, or watching* Flip This House *(if she's got the remote) or* The Golden Girls *(if he does), or else having dinner at the all-you-can-eat rib buffet and dessert at Dairy Queen.*[7]

In response to the repeated rumors that they're starting a family, both Shelton and Lambert insist this is not a good time for them to have children, given that their work schedules have them traveling so frequently. "We're so busy. It's this whole whirlwind right now, flying all over the place, and we'd like to be a little more settled."[8] Shelton's goals are simple: "Do well enough to spend a lot more time in Tishomingo with Miranda; keep the possums out of my watermelon patch, my deer stand in good repair and the local taxidermist busy with lunker large mouth bass and eight-point bucks; and patronize the local beer joints."[9] And no matter where his career takes him, and no matter how often he's on the road, the country is where his heart is, far away from the glitter and paparazzi of the cities and the celebrity life. Shelton's hillbilly bone will always bring him home again.

||||||||||

"I've realized after ten years that I do know a lot of stuff, whether I like it or not. I have turned into a wise old music pro man."[10]

—BLAKE SHELTON ON TEN YEARS IN THE COUNTRY MUSIC BUSINESS

Shelton and Lambert in 2013

TIMELINE

1976

Blake Tollison Shelton is born in Ada, Oklahoma, on June 18.

1990

Shelton's older brother, Richie, dies in a car accident on November 13.

1994

Shelton graduates from high school and moves to Nashville, Tennessee.

2004

Shelton releases his third album, *Blake Shelton's Barn & Grill*.

2005

Shelton meets Miranda Lambert when they perform together on CMT's 100 Greatest Duets concert.

2006

Shelton and Williams divorce.

1998

2001

2003

Shelton signs with
Giant Records.

Shelton's first album,
Blake Shelton,
and his debut
single, "Austin,"
are released.

Shelton marries
Kaynette Williams
on November 17.

2007

2007

2010

Shelton releases
his fourth album,
Pure BS.

Shelton appears
as a judge on the
TV show *Nashville
Star,* and also on
Clash of the Choirs.

Shelton is invited
to join the Grand
Ole Opry and is
formally inducted
on October 23.

TIMELINE

2011

2011

2011

Shelton marries
Miranda Lambert
on May 14.

Shelton joins the
television show
The Voice as a
judge and coach.

Shelton releases
his album *Red
River Blue*.

2013

2013

2013

Shelton releases his
eighth album, *Based
on a True Story . . .*

During the
2013 Academy
of Country Music
Awards, Shelton
wins the Gene
Weed Special
Achievement Award.

Shelton organizes
and performs at
the Healing in the
Heartland concert
to benefit Oklahoma
tornado victims.

2012

2012

2012

Shelton's father, Richard Shelton, dies in Oklahoma on January 17.

Shelton and Lambert sing during the halftime of Super Bowl XLVI.

Shelton releases his Christmas album, *Cheers, It's Christmas*.

2014

2014

2014

Shelton and Lambert appear in the Academy of Country Music Salute to the Troops concert.

Shelton's tour dates at the Hollywood Bowl and Madison Square Garden sell out.

Shelton and Lambert open a bed-and-breakfast in their hometown of Tishomingo, Oklahoma.

GET THE SCOOP

FULL NAME

Blake Tollison Shelton

DATE OF BIRTH

June 18, 1976

PLACE OF BIRTH

Ada, Oklahoma

MARRIAGES

Kaynette Williams (November 17, 2003–2006)

Miranda Lambert (May 14, 2011–)

ALBUMS

Blake Shelton (2001), *The Dreamer* (2003), *Blake Shelton's Barn & Grill* (2004), *Pure BS* (2007), *Startin' Fires* (2008), *Red River Blue* (2011), *Cheers, It's Christmas* (2012), *Based on a True Story. . .* (2013), *Bringing Back the Sunshine* (2014)

TELEVISION APPEARANCES

Nashville Star, Clash of the Choirs, The Voice

SELECTED AWARDS

- Record for consecutive Number 1 country single hits
- 2012 CMA Entertainer of the Year, Song of the Year, and Male Vocalist of the Year
- Recipient of the 2013 Gene Weed Special Achievement Award

PHILANTHROPY

Shelton helped organize the Healing in the Heartland concert to benefit the victims of the 2013 Oklahoma tornadoes. He also regularly does benefit concerts and travels with the USO.

"For the life of me, I'll never understand how you can be an artist but not want people to understand who you are as a person."

—BLAKE SHELTON ON HIS PHILOSOPHY AS AN ARTIST

GLOSSARY

Billboard—A music chart system used by the music recording industry to measure record popularity and sales.

brevity—The shortness of time.

debut—A first appearance.

endorsement—The act of recommending a product, such as in an ad, often in return for payment.

genre—A category of art, music, or literature characterized by a particular style, form, or content.

Grammy Award—One of several awards the National Academy of Recording Arts and Sciences presents each year to honor musical achievement.

induct—To formally admit someone to a position or organization.

lucrative—Making a profit or producing wealth.

mentor—A person with experience in a specific field, who guides someone with less experience.

motocross—The sport of racing motorcycles over a rough course with many hills and sharp turns.

nominee—A person who is formally proposed as a possible winner of an award.

obliterate—Completely destroyed, wiped out, or demolished.

prestigious—Important or highly respected.

producer—Someone who oversees or provides money for a play, television show, movie, or album.

single—An individual song that is distributed on its own over the radio and other mediums.

tabloid—A newspaper or magazine that publishes sensational stories, often about celebrities.

ADDITIONAL RESOURCES

SELECTED BIBLIOGRAPHY

"Blake Shelton, Coach." *NBC*. NBC Universal, 2014. Web. 5 June 2014.

BlakeShelton.com. Warner Music Nashville, n.d. Web. 4 June 2014.

Eaton, Keith. "Blake Shelton: An Oklahoma Original Is Singing His Way Back Home." *Distinctly Oklahoma*. Distinctly Oklahoma Magazine, 4 Oct. 2010. Web. 30 May 2014.

Eells, Josh. "Blake Shelton, Natural Born Hell-Raiser." *Men's Journal*. Men's Journal LLC, Aug. 2013. Web. 5 June 2014.

FURTHER READINGS

Carlin, Richard. *American Popular Music: Country*. New York: Facts on File, 2005. Print.

Shackleford, Dorothy, and Travis Thrasher. *Time for Me to Come Home*. New York: New American Library, 2013. Print.

Tieck, Sarah. *Blake Shelton: Country Music Star*. Minneapolis: Abdo, 2013. Print.

WEBSITES

To learn more about Contemporary Lives, visit **booklinks.abdopublishing.com**. These links are routinely monitored and updated to provide the most current information available.

PLACES TO VISIT

Country Music Hall of Fame and Museum
222 Fifth Avenue South
Nashville, TN 37203
http://countrymusichalloffame.org
615-416-2001
Learn more about country music through artifacts and interactive exhibits in the hall of fame and museum.

The Grand Ole Opry
2804 Opryland Drive
Nashville, TN 37214
http://www.opry.com
615-871-6779
The Grand Ole Opry is a weekly country music stage concert in Nashville. Many of the biggest country artists, including Blake Shelton, have performed here.

Musicians Hall of Fame & Museum
401 Gay Street
Nashville, TN 37201
http://www.musicianshalloffame.com
615-244-3263
The Musicians Hall of Fame & Museum honors musicians from all genres. Visit the timeline to learn more about the history of recorded music.

SOURCE NOTES

CHAPTER 1. A NIGHT OF AWARDS

1. "Blake Shelton Miranda Lambert—Win Song of the Year 'Over You'—CMA Awards 2012." *YouTube.com*. YouTube, 1 Nov. 2012. Web. 25 July 2014.

2. Ibid.

3. Alanna Conaway. "Miranda Lambert, 'Over You'—Lyrics Uncovered." *Taste of Country*. Taste of Country Network, 2 July 2012. Web. 25 July 2014.

4. Josh Eells. "Blake Shelton, Natural Born Hell-Raiser." *Men's Journal*. Men's Journal LLC, Aug. 2013. Web. 25 July 2014.

5. "History of the Awards." *RIAA*. RIAA, n.d. Web. 25 July 2014.

6. Billy Dukes. "10 Things You Didn't Know about Blake Shelton." *Taste of Country*. Taste of Country Network, n.d. Web. 25 July 2014.

CHAPTER 2. A BOY FROM OKLAHOMA

1. Dyrinda Tyson. "Team Blake." *Oklahoma Today*. Oklahoma Today, Sept./Oct. 2011. Web. 25 July 2014.

2. Billy Dukes. "10 Things You Didn't Know about Blake Shelton." *Taste of Country*. Taste of Country Network, n.d. Web. 25 July 2014.

3. Dyrinda Tyson. "Team Blake." *Oklahoma Today*. Oklahoma Today, Sept./Oct. 2011. Web. 25 July 2014.

4. "Blake Shelton Opens Up about His Late Brother, Richie." *WWGP AM1050 Today's Best Country*. WWGP Broadcasting Corp., 12 July 2013. Web. 25 July 2014.

5. Billy Dukes. "Blake Shelton Talks about Fatal Accident That Inspired Miranda Lambert's 'Over You.'" *Taste of Country*. Taste of Country Network, 12 Dec. 2011. Web. 25 July 2014.

6. Dyrinda Tyson. "Team Blake." *Oklahoma Today*. Oklahoma Today, Sept./Oct. 2011. Web. 25 July 2014.

7. Keith Eaton. "Blake Shelton: An Oklahoma Original Is Singing His Way Back Home." *Distinctly Oklahoma*. Distinctly Oklahoma Magazine, 4 Oct. 2010. Web. 25 July 2014.

8. Ibid.

9. Dyrinda Tyson. "Team Blake." *Oklahoma Today*. Oklahoma Today, Sept./Oct. 2011. Web. 25 July 2014.

10. Ibid.

CHAPTER 3. MAKING HIS WAY TO THE TOP

1. Robert L Doerschuk. "Review of *The Dreamer*." *AllMusic*. AllMusic, n.d. Web. 25 July 2014.

2. "Concert Review—Shock 'N Y'all Tour." *About.com*. About.com, n.d. Web. 25 July 2014.

3. Billy Dukes. "10 Things You Didn't Know about Blake Shelton." *Taste of Country*. Taste of Country Network, n.d. Web. 25 July 2014.

4. Wendy Newcomer. "Chapel of Love." *Country Weekly*. American Media, 16 Dec. 2003. Web. 25 July 2014.

5. Gayle Thompson. "Miranda Lambert Knew Blake Shelton Was Initially 'Off-Limits.'" *The Boot*. Taste of Country Network, 30 Aug. 2011. Web. 25 July 2014.

6. Ibid.

7. Ibid.

CHAPTER 4. *STARTIN' FIRES* AND MORE

1. Dyrinda Tyson. "Team Blake." *Oklahoma Today*. Oklahoma Today, Sept./Oct. 2011. Web. 25 July 2014.

2. Amy Sciattetto. "Miranda Lambert Dishes on How Blake Shelton Proposed." *Taste of Country*. Taste of Country Network, 18 Nov. 2011. Web. 25 July 2014.

3. "Blake Shelton Proposes to Miranda Lambert in 'Old-School' Way." *AceShowbiz*. AceShowbiz.com, 12 May 2010. Web. 25 July 2014.

4. Michelle Tauber, Danielle Anderson, and Eileen Finan. "Miranda Lambert & Blake Shelton Wedding Album." *People*. Time Inc., 6 July 2011. Web. 25 July 2014.

5. Ibid.

6. Billy Dukes. "10 Things You Didn't Know about Blake Shelton." *Taste of Country*. Taste of Country Network, n.d. Web. 25 July 2014.

7. "Blake Shelton Has a Record-Breaking Week." *All Access Music Group*. All Access Music Group, 13 Apr. 2011. Web. 29 July 2014.

8. "Blake Shelton Is No. 1 in America!" *Warner Music Nashville*. Warner Music Nashville, 20 July 2011. Web. 25 July 2014.

9. "About Blake Shelton." *CMT Artists*. Viacom International, n.d. Web. 25 July 2014.

CHAPTER 5. *THE VOICE*

1. Josh Eells. "Blake Shelton, Natural Born Hell-Raiser." *Men's Journal*. Men's Journal LLC, Aug. 2013. Web. 25 July 2014.

2. Gayle Thompson. "Blake Shelton Speaks Out after 'Lord' Removed from Gospel Song on 'The Voice.'" *The Boot*. Taste of Country Network, 3 Dec. 2013. Web. 25 July 2014.

3. Brittany Frederick. "Why 'The Voice' Can't Lose Adam Levine and Blake Shelton." *Starpulse.com*. Starpulse.com, 5 Apr. 2014. Web. 28 July 2014.

4. Alison Bonaguro. "Offstage: Top 10 Blake Shelton Quotes from *The Voice*." *CMT*. Country Music Television, 10 May 2012. Web. 28 July 2014.

5. "Blake Shelton Bought Dia Frampton's Phillip Lim Dress She Wore on 'The Voice' Finale." *Hollywood Life*. PMC, 30 June 2011. Web. 28 July 2014.

6. Dyrinda Tyson. "Team Blake." *Oklahoma Today*. Oklahoma Today, Sept./Oct. 2011. Web. 25 July 2014.

7. Drusilla Moorhouse. "Blake Shelton Tweets Adam Levine's Phone Number during 'The Voice.'" *TODAY*. NBCNews.com, 29 Apr. 2014. Web. 28 July 2014.

8. Brittany Frederick. "Why 'The Voice' Can't Lose Adam Levine and Blake Shelton." *Starpulse.com*. Starpulse.com, 5 Apr. 2014. Web. 28 July 2014.

CHAPTER 6. IN THE PUBLIC EYE

1. Josh Eells. "Blake Shelton, Natural Born Hell-Raiser." *Men's Journal*. Men's Journal LLC, Aug. 2013. Web. 25 July 2014.

2. Tim Nudd. "Blake Shelton's Father Dies." *People*. Time Inc., 18 Jan. 2012. Web. 28 July 2014.

3. Josh Eells. "Blake Shelton, Natural Born Hell-Raiser." *Men's Journal*. Men's Journal LLC, Aug. 2013. Web. 25 July 2014.

4. "Blake Shelton Is Country's Entertainer of the Year." *Warner Music Nashville*. Warner Music Nashville, 3 Nov. 2012. Web. 28 July 2014.

5. "Blake Shelton Calls Classic Country Fans 'Old Farts' and 'Jackasses.'" *Saving Country Music.com*. Saving Country Music, 23 Jan. 2013. Web. 28 July 2014.

CHAPTER 7. *BASED ON A TRUE STORY* . . .

1. "Blake Shelton's Based on a True Story...Debuts At No. 1." *Warner Music Nashville*. Warner Music Nashville, 3 Apr. 2013. Web. 28 July 2014.

2. Wendy Newcomer. "Jason Aldean, Guy Clark, Blake Shelton & More Announced as ACM Awards Off-Camera Winners." *Great American Country*. Scripps Networks, 22 Mar. 2013. Web. 28 July 2014.

3. Chuck Dauphin. "Blake Shelton, Jason Aldean and Lady Antebellum Embrace ACM Honors." *Billboard*. Billboard, 12 Sept. 2013. Web. 28 July 2014.

4. "Blake Shelton's Ten Times Crazier Tour Kicks Off Tomorrow, July 19." *Warner Music Nashville*. Warner Music Nashville, 18 July 2013. Web. 28 July 2014.

5. "Blake Shelton's 'Ten Times Crazier' Tour Sells Out First Two Weekends." *Warner Music Nashville*. Warner Music Nashville, 22 July 2013. Web. 28 July 2014.

6. Eileen Finan and Kay West. "Miranda Lambert Opens Up about Turning 30 and Life in the Spotlight." *People*. Time Inc., 25 Mar. 2014. Web. 28 July 2014.

7. Rachel Maresca. "Blake Shelton, Miranda Lambert Laugh Off More Split Rumors: 'We're Reading about Our Separation.'" *Daily News*. NYDailyNews.com, 17 Apr. 2014. Web. 28 July 2014.

8. Alison Bonaguro. "Blake Shelton Again Dispels Divorce Rumors." *CMT*. Country Music Television, 22 Apr. 2014. Web. 28 July 2014.

9. Dyrinda Tyson. "Team Blake." *Oklahoma Today*. Oklahoma Today, Sept./Oct. 2011. Web. 25 July 2014.

CHAPTER 8. HEALING IN THE HEARTLAND

1. "Moore, Okla. Tornado Death Toll Rises." *The Weather Channel*. The Weather Channel, 5 Aug. 2013. Web. 29 July 2014.

2. "Fujita Tornado Damage Scale." *NOAA's National Weather Service*. National Weather Service, n.d. Web. 28 July 2014.

3. Josh Eells. "Blake Shelton, Natural Born Hell-Raiser." *Men's Journal*. Men's Journal LLC, Aug. 2013. Web. 25 July 2014.

4. Bob Paxman. "Blake Shelton's 'Healing in the Heartland' Raises $6 Million for Tornado Victims." *Country Weekly*. American Media, 31 May 2013. Web. 29 July 2014.

5. Eric R. Danton. "Blake Shelton, Usher Sing 'Home' at Oklahoma Benefit Concert." *Rolling Stone*. Rolling Stone, 30 May 2013. Web. 28 July 2014.

6. Jessica Nicholson. "Shelton Works With JCPenney to Support USO." *MusicRow*. MusicRow, 20 Dec. 2013. Web. 29 July 2014.

7. "Blake Shelton Announces Ten Times Crazier Tour." *Warner Music Nashville*. Warner Music Nashville, 17 Jan. 2012. Web. 28 July 2014.

8. "Blake Shelton." *People*. Time Inc., n.d. Web. 28 July 2014.

9. "Blake Shelton Sells Out Madison Square Garden and Hollywood Bowl." *Warner Music Nashville*. Warner Music Nashville, 7 Mar. 2014. Web. 28 July 2014.

CHAPTER 9. LOOKING FORWARD

1. Keith Eaton. "Blake Shelton: An Oklahoma Original Is Singing His Way Back Home." *Distinctly Oklahoma*. Distinctly Oklahoma Magazine, 4 Oct. 2010. Web. 25 July 2014.

2. "Blake Shelton Bio." *Blake Shelton.com*. Blake Shelton, n.d. Web. 28 2014.

3. Josh Eells. "Blake Shelton, Natural Born Hell-Raiser." *Men's Journal*. Men's Journal LLC, Aug. 2013. Web. 25 July 2014.

4. Scott T. Sterling. "Blake Shelton Is the Face of Pizza Hut's New Line of Barbecue Pies." *Radio.com*. CBS Local Media, 8 May 2014. Web. 28 July 2014.

5. Coti Howell. "'Oklahoma Stuffer' Amongst Rejected Blake Shelton Pizza Names." *Taste of Country*. Taste of Country Network, 23 May 2014. Web. 28 July 2014.

6. Dyrinda Tyson. "Team Blake." *Oklahoma Today*. Oklahoma Today, Sept./Oct. 2011. Web. 25 July 2014.

7. Josh Eells. "Blake Shelton, Natural Born Hell-Raiser." *Men's Journal*. Men's Journal LLC, Aug. 2013. Web. 25 July 2014.

8. Carrie Horton. "Miranda Lambert's Cure for Baby Fever: 'I Get a Puppy.'" *Taste of Country*. Taste of Country Network, 10 Apr. 2014. Web. 28 July 2014.

9. Keith Eaton. "Blake Shelton: An Oklahoma Original Is Singing His Way Back Home." *Distinctly Oklahoma*. Distinctly Oklahoma Magazine, 4 Oct. 2010. Web. 25 July 2014.

10. Dyrinda Tyson. "Team Blake." *Oklahoma Today*. Oklahoma Today, Sept./Oct. 2011. Web. 25 July 2014.

INDEX

ABOUT THE AUTHOR

Marcia Amidon Lusted is the author of more than 95 books for young readers and hundreds of magazine articles. She is also the editor of *AppleSeeds* magazine, a writing instructor, and a musician. She lives in New Hampshire.